TRADITIONS AND CELEBRATIONS

CINCO DE MAYO

by Sharon Katz Cooper

PEBBLE
a capstone imprint

Pebble Explore is published by Pebble, an imprint of Capstone.
1710 Roe Crest Drive
North Mankato, Minnesota 56003
www.capstonepub.com

Library of Congress Cataloging-in-Publication Data
Names: Katz Cooper, Sharon, author.
Title: Cinco de Mayo / by Sharon Katz Cooper.
Description: North Mankato, Minnesota : Pebble Explore, 2021. | Series: Traditions and celebrations | Includes bibliographical references and index. | Audience: Ages 6-8 | Audience: Grades 2-3 |
Summary: "Cinco de Mayo is about celebrating! It honors a Mexican Army victory during the Battle of Puebla in 1862. Some people mark the holiday with folk dancing or traditional foods such as chalupas and mole poblano. Others watch parades or attend cultural festivals. Readers will discover how a shared holiday can have multiple traditions and be celebrated in all sorts of ways"—Provided by publisher.
Identifiers: LCCN 2020038009 (print) | LCCN 2020038010 (ebook) | ISBN 9781977131850 (hardcover) | ISBN 9781977132871 (paperback) | ISBN 9781977154019 (pdf) | ISBN 9781977155726 (kindle edition)
Subjects: LCSH: Cinco de Mayo (Mexican holiday)—Juvenile literature. | Mexico—Social life and customs—Juvenile literature. Classification: LCC F1233 .K28 2021 (print) | LCC F1233 (ebook) | DDC 394.262—dc23
LC record available at https://lccn.loc.gov/2020038009
LC ebook record available at https://lccn.loc.gov/2020038010

Image Credits
Alamy: agefotostock, 7; Getty Images: Daniel Zuchnik/Contributor, 28, Jeff Greenberg/Contributor, 16, Luis Sinco/Contributor, 21, Star Tribune via Getty Images, 13, Susana Gonzalez/Stringer, 8; iStockphoto: DOUGBERRY, 19, Ryan Rahman, 26, 27; Newscom: Bryan Smith/ZUMA Press, 29, RICHARD B. LEVINE, 9, SAMANTHA SAIS/Reuters, 25; Shutterstock: bonchan, 14, Brent Hofacker, 15 (right), Esdelval, 11, Guajillo studio, 10, kdbphoto, 17, Kit Leong, 4, 24, MobileSaint, 5, nelea33, 15 (left), Peter Titmuss, 1, Roberto Galan, 22, 23, Shiela Fitzgerald, 18, Simon Hogan, cover

Artistic elements: Shutterstock/Rafal Kulik

Editorial Credits
Editor: Jill Kalz; Designer: Juliette Peters; Media Researcher: Kelly Garvin; Production Specialist: Spencer Rosio

Consultant
Isela Xitlali Gómez

All internet sites appearing in back matter were available and accurate when this book was sent to press.

TABLE OF CONTENTS

WHAT IS
CINCO DE MAYO?......................4

IN MEXICO.................................. 8

IN THE UNITED STATES........... 12

CITY CELEBRATIONS.............. 20

GLOSSARY 30

READ MORE 31

INTERNET SITES...................31

INDEX 32

HOW TO SAY IT................... 32

Words in **bold** are in the glossary.

WHAT IS CINCO DE MAYO?

Cinco de Mayo is a day to **celebrate**. It comes from Mexico. It happens on May 5. *Cinco de Mayo* means "fifth of May" in Spanish.

This special day honors an important battle in Mexico's past. It celebrates that Mexico won.

The battle happened in 1862. French soldiers had charged into Mexico in late 1861. They marched to the city of Puebla. On May 5, 1862, a battle broke out. French soldiers fought Mexican soldiers.

The French had more soldiers. They had a strong army. They had better weapons. The French expected an easy win.

But the Mexican soldiers were tough. They fought hard and beat the French.

IN MEXICO

More than 300,000 people go to Puebla every year for Cinco de Mayo. Some dress as French or Mexican soldiers. On May 5, they put on a show. They pretend to fight. The Mexican soldiers always win. Then everyone celebrates!

The city has a parade with colorful **floats**. **Folklórico** dancers wear bright clothes. They dance in the streets. There are fireworks too.

People eat tasty food on Cinco de Mayo. A dish called chile relleno comes from Puebla. It is made from green chili peppers. The peppers are stuffed with cheese and then fried.

Many cooks enter contests. They try to make the best mole poblano. Mole is a thick brown sauce. It has spices, chili peppers, and chocolate in it. People pour the sauce over chicken, turkey, enchiladas, and more.

IN THE UNITED STATES

In the United States, Cinco de Mayo means something different. It is a day to celebrate Mexican **culture**. Mexican Americans and **Chicanos** show pride for their history.

Many U.S. cities have Cinco de Mayo events. People enjoy Mexican food and drinks. They dance and listen to music. There are **salsa**-tasting contests and carnival rides. People display their **low-rider** cars in parades and car shows.

Food is a big part of the celebration. Tacos are a popular food. People also eat other Mexican foods. Ceviche, churros, and empanadas are a few of them.

Ceviche

Churros

Empanadas

Ceviche is raw seafood with lemon or lime juice. Churros are fried tubes of dough. The tubes are rolled in cinnamon and sugar. Empanadas are baked or fried dumplings. They are filled with meat, cheese, vegetables, or sweet fillings.

What goes well with Mexican food? Mexican drinks! On Cinco de Mayo, kids enjoy drinking agua frescas. The name means "fresh water" or "cool water" in Spanish. These cold drinks are made of water and fruit. Melon, pineapple, **tamarind**, and cucumber are common flavors.

Kids of all ages enjoy Mexican ice pops called paletas. There are many flavors to choose from. Try strawberry or coconut. How about chili, carrot, or shrimp?

Many women wear long dresses at Cinco de Mayo events. The dresses have bright colors. They twirl when the women dance. Men wear hats with wide brims. The hats are called sombreros.

Mariachi bands play. Mariachi is a kind of Mexican music. It is played by a group. Band members play violins, trumpets, or guitars. Some members also sing.

CITY CELEBRATIONS

Los Angeles, California, has the largest Cinco de Mayo celebration in the world. It is called Fiesta Broadway. Workers turn the city red, white, and green. Those colors make up the Mexican flag.

People give speeches in Spanish and English. They speak about culture, pride, and **immigration** rights. Others tell folktales. Folktales are important to Mexican culture. Bands play. Guests meet famous Chicano people too.

The Cinco de Mayo event in Chicago, Illinois, lasts for days. Many places serve Mexican food and drinks. People sell or shop for handmade crafts. They take Mexican dance lessons or listen to bands.

The event ends with a big parade. Floats, dancers, and horseback riders called charros fill the streets. The parade is a **tradition** for many families each year.

People in Denver, Colorado, also celebrate Cinco de Mayo. They dance and listen to music. They watch a parade. Kids have their own play area. Hundreds of food sellers offer tacos, churros, and other Mexican treats.

Two events are extra special. One is a green-chili cooking contest. The other is a **Chihuahua** race! Anyone can enter their little dog and cheer it on.

New York City celebrates Cinco de Mayo in a big way. Its parade goes right through the city. Music fills the air. Folklórico dancers dance in the streets. People on the sidewalks dance too. Some wave Mexican flags. Others sing along with the music.

New Yorkers have many big street fairs. The Cinco de Mayo street fair is free and fun! Families spend the day listening to Mexican stories. They shop for arts and crafts. They eat tacos and corn.

People celebrate Cinco de Mayo in many ways. No matter how it's celebrated, the day is fun for all!

GLOSSARY

celebrate (SEL-uh-brayt)—to do something fun on a special day

Chicano (chi-CAH-noh)—an American of Mexican descent

Chihuahua (chi-WAH-WAH)—the smallest type of dog, named after a Mexican state

culture (KUL-chur)—a people's way of life, ideas, art, customs, and traditions

float (FLOHT)—a decorated truck or flat wagon that is part of a parade

folklórico (fohl-KLOR-ee-koh)—traditional Latin American dances that emphasize local folk culture

immigration (im-uh-GRAY-shun)—the act of moving to another country to live

low-rider (LOW-rye-duhr)—a car with a body that has been lowered

salsa (SALL-sah)—a sauce made with tomatoes, onions, and spices

tamarind (TA-muh-rihnd)—the sweet, brown, pod-like fruit from the tamarind tree

tradition (tra-DIH-shun)—a custom, idea, or belief passed down through time

READ MORE

Berne, Emma Carlson. *Cinco de Mayo*. North Mankato, MN: Cantata Learning, 2018.

Murray, Julie. *Cinco de Mayo*. Minneapolis: Abdo Kids Junior, 2019.

Sebra, Richard. *It's Cinco de Mayo!* Minneapolis: Lerner Publications, 2017.

INTERNET SITES

Cinco de Mayo
britannica.com/topic/Cinco-de-Mayo

Cinco de Mayo: All About the Holidays
pbslearningmedia.org/resource/84c2b3ff-131c-432d-8f96-78e88971b629/cinco-de-mayo-all-about-the-holidays/

Cinco de Mayo: Fiesta Fun!
kids.nationalgeographic.com/explore/history/cinco-de-mayo/

INDEX

battle, 5–6, 8

clothing, 8–9, 18
contests, 11, 12, 25

dancing, 9, 12, 18, 22–24, 26
date, 4

folktales, 20
foods, 10–11, 12, 14–17, 22, 24–25, 28
France, 6, 8

history, 5–6, 12

Mexican flag, 20, 26
music, 12, 19, 20, 22, 24, 26

parades, 9, 12, 23–24, 26
Puebla, Mexico, 6, 8, 10

speeches, 20
street fairs, 28

U.S. celebrations, 20, 22–26, 28

HOW TO SAY IT

agua fresca
    (AH-gwah FRES-kah)
ceviche
    (seh-VEE-cheh)
charro
    (CHAH-rroh)
chile relleno
    (CHEE-leh reh-yeh-noh)
churro
    (choo-rroh)
Cinco de Mayo
    (SEEN-koh deh MY-oh)

empanada
    (em-pa-NAH-dah)
enchilada
    (en-cheh-LAH-dah)
mariachi
    (mah-RREE-AH-chee)
mole poblano
    (MOH-leh poh-BLAH-noh)
paleta
    (pah-LEH-tah)
sombrero
    (som-breh-rroh)